The Gospel In 3-D!

The End
of All Distance,
Delay, & Dispute!

Part 1

Rudi Louw

Table of Contents

The Marvel of the Holy Bible

1. Uninterrupted Theme and Inspired Thought

It took *1,500 years* to compile the Holy Bible, involving *more than 40 different authors*. <u>Yet</u> the theme and inspired thought of Scripture continues *uninterrupted* from author to author, from beginning till end.

2. Absence of Mythical Stories

Compare philosophies and theories about creation in the Middle East, Europe, Asia, Africa, and Latin America and you'll find mythical scenarios: gods feuding and cutting up other gods to form the heavens and the earth, etc.

In ancient Greek mythology, the Greeks see Atlas carrying the earth on his shoulders. In India, Hindus believe eight elephants carry the earth on their backs.

But in contrast, Job, the oldest book in the Holy Bible, declares that, *"God suspends the earth on nothing."(Job 26:7)*

This was said millennia before Isaac Newton discovered the invisible laws of gravity that delicately balance every planet and sun in its individual circuit.

Contrary to every other ancient attempt to give a creation account, *the Holy Bible pictures the creation of the earth in a very scientific manner.*

For example, in Genesis Chapter One, the continents are lifted from the seas, then vegetation is formed and later animal life, all reproducing *'according to its own kind',* **thus recognizing the fixed genetic laws.** In addition, we have the bringing forth of man and woman, *all done by God in a dignified and proper manner, without mythological adornments.*

The balance or remainder of the Holy Bible follows suite.

The narratives are **true historical documents**, *faithfully reflecting society and culture* **as history and archaeology would discover them thousands of years later. Not only is the Holy Bible historically accurate, it is also reliable when it deals with scientifically proven subjects.**

It was never intended to be a textbook on history, science, mathematics, or medicine. *However, when its writers touch on these subjects,* **they often state facts that scientific advancement would not reveal, or** *even consider, until thousands of years later.*

While many have questioned the accuracy of the Holy Bible, and can even prove some inconsistencies, *time and continued research have demonstrated again and again that the Bible's theme and inspired thought; its message: The Word of God is indeed better informed than its critics.*

3. Durability

Of all the ancient works of substantial size, *the Holy Bible survives intact, against all odds and expectations.*

Compared with other ancient writings, the Holy Bible has more manuscripts as evidence to support it than any ten pieces of classical literature combined!

The plays of William Shakespeare, for instance, were written about four hundred years ago, after the invention of the printing press. Many of his original writings and words have been lost in numerous sections, *yet the Holy Bible's uncanny preservation has weathered thousands of years of wars, contradictions, persecutions, fires and invasions.*

Through the centuries Jewish scribes have preserved the Holy Bible's Old Covenant text, **such as no other manuscripts have ever**

been preserved. They kept track of every letter, syllable, word and paragraph; *preserving the text continuously from generation to generation. Special groups of me within their culture were appointed and trained. It was their sole duty to preserve and transmit these documents* **with perfect accuracy and fidelity**.

So, besides a few provable inconsistencies, it is indeed astonishing just how accurately the Holy Bible has been preserved!

Who ever bothered to count the letters, syllables, or words of Plato, Aristotle, or Seneca for that matter?

As to the New Testament, the actual number of preserved manuscripts is so great that it becomes overwhelming. **There are more than 5,680 Greek manuscripts, more than 10,000 Latin Vulgate manuscripts and at least 9,300 other versions. Further still, there exists an additional 25,000 manuscript copies of portions of the New Testament. Each one of these is in extremely close agreement with the others.** No other document of antiquity even begins to approach such numbers.

The closest in comparison is Homer's Iliad, with only 643 manuscripts. The first complete work of Homer only dates back to the 13th century.

4. Unmatched Accuracy in Predictive Foretelling

The Holy Bible is unmatched in accuracy in predictive foretelling. No other ancient work succeeds in this, or even begins to attempt this.

Other books such as the Koran, the Book of Mormon, and parts of the Veda claim divine inspiration; *but none of these books contain predictive foretelling.*

This one undeniable fact we know for certain: *While <u>microscopic scrutiny</u> would show up the imperfections, blemishes, and defects of any work of Man (including the actual penning down of the Scriptures), yet, <u>it magnifies the beauties and perfection of God</u>. Just as every flower displays in accurate detail the reflection and perfection of beauty, <u>so does the Word of Truth revealed in Christ when it is scrutinized</u>.*

Historian Philip Schaff wrote:

"Without money and weapons, Jesus the Christ conquered more millions than Alexander, Caesar, Muhammad, and Napoleon. Without science and learning, He (Jesus the Christ) shed more light on things human and divine than all philosophers and scholars combined. Without the eloquence of schools, He (Jesus the Christ) spoke such words of life as was never spoken before or

since and produced effects which lie beyond the reach of orator or poet. Without writing a single line, He (Jesus the Christ) set more pens in motion and furnished themes for more sermons, orations, discussions, learned volumes, works of art, and songs of praise **than the whole army of great men of ancient and modern times combined.**" (*The Person of Christ*, p33. 1913)

Today, there are literally billions of Bibles in more than 2,000 languages, and although there is no perfect translation; *there is a perfect Word:* Isn't it about time you find out *what that Word really has to say?*

Hey listen, the Holy Bible is all about Jesus, the Messiah, the Christ…

…and everything about Jesus Christ is really about YOU!!

Study Tips:

Read 2 Corinthians 5:14, 16, 18, 19, and 21.

In the light of these Scriptures, it should be obvious that, if you want to study the Holy Bible, *you should study it in the light of Mankind's redemption! Feed daily on* **redemption realities** found in the book of Acts, in Romans Chapters 1 through 8, in Ephesians, Colossians, Galatians, and in 1 Peter Chapter 1, 2 Peter Chapter 1, James Chapter 1, as well as in 1 and 2 Corinthians.

Acknowledgment

I want to acknowledge and thank one of my mentors in the faith, Francois du Toit, for blessing and impacting me with revelation knowledge.

I borrowed the portion on *"The Marvel of the Holy Bible"* from his website: http://www.MirrorWord.net, as students so often feel they have a right to do with things that come from teachers they respect. Just as Galatians 6:6 says, *"Let him who is taught the Word **share in all good things** with him who teaches."*

To all our dear friends and family, for all the love and support, and to all those who helped me with this project:

THANK YOU!

Also, especially to my wife, Carmen;

For keeping me real by being my companion in life and partner in ministry,

I love and appreciate you so very much!

Foreword

Thank you for taking the time to read this book.

Let me start off by saying that *I am in love with Jesus Christ; through Him I have become totally addicted to my Daddy's love for me, and that is enough for me!*

The love of God is so much more than a doctrine, a philosophy, or a theory. It is so much more and goes so much deeper than knowledge; *it way surpasses knowledge.* **We are talking heart language here.**

Thus, I write **to impact people's hearts,** to make them see the mysteries that have been hidden in Father God's heart concerning Christ Jesus, and actually *concerning THEM,* so as to arrest their conscience with it, *that I may introduce them to their original design and to their true selves, to their ultimate selves,* **and present them to themselves perfect in Christ Jesus** *and set them apart unto Him* **in love,** as a chaste virgin.

We are involved with the biggest romance of the ages. Therefore this book cannot be read as you would a novel: *casually.* It is not a cleverly devised little myth or fable. **It contains revelation into some things, and thus** *truth* **you may or may not have considered before.**

It is *the very TRUTH of God, ultimate TRUTH, and therefore has direct bearing upon YOUR life.* The Word and the Spirit are my witness *to the REALITY of these things!*

Be like the people of Berea the apostle Paul ministered to in Acts 17:11. Open yourself up to study the revelation contained in this book *to discover for yourself the REALITY of these things*.

Be forewarned! Do not become guilty of the sins of the Pharisees, **or you too will miss out on** <u>**the depth of fulfillment**</u> **God Himself, who is LOVE, wants to give you***.*

Jesus said of the Pharisees and Sadducee that they strain out every little gnat BUT swallow whole camels. What He meant by that is that *some people seem to have it all together when it comes to doctrine and they love to argue.* **It makes them feel important, but it is nothing other than EMPTY religious and intellectual pride.** *They know the Scriptures in and out, and YET they are still so IGNORANT about* **REAL TRUTH that is only found in LOVE;** *They are always arguing over the use of every little jot and tittle and over the meaning and interpretation of every word of Scripture, but they are still so ignorant and indifferent* **towards the things that REALLY MATTER!**

The exact thing they accuse everyone else of doing though, the precise thing they judge everyone else for, *they are actually doing themselves.* That is **they often downright misinterpret and twist what is being said, *making a big deal of insignificant things while obscuring or weakening God's real truth: the truth of His LOVE.***

*They are always majoring on minors **<u>because they do not understand the heart of God</u>** and therefore they constantly miss the whole point of the message.*

Paul himself said it so beautifully,

*"...the letter kills but **the Spirit BRINGS LIFE**;"*
- 2 Corinthians 3:6

*"...<u>knowledge puffs up</u>, but **LOVE EDIFIES**."*
- 1 Corinthians 8:1

I say again: *Allow yourself to get caught up in the revelation I am about to share. Open yourself up to study the insight contained in this book, not only with a desire to gain knowledge, but also with anticipation **to hear from Father God yourself, to encounter Him through His Word, and to embrace truth, in order to know and believe the LOVE God has for <u>YOU</u>, and to then get so caught up in it that you too may receive from Him LOVE's impartation of LIFE.***

The message contained in the gospel and revealed in this book also, is indeed the very voice and call of LOVE Himself to every human being on the face of this earth. If you do take

15

heed to it, it is custom designed and guaranteed **to forever alter and enrich your life!**

"The kingdom of heaven

is like
TREASURE

HIDDEN

in an agricultural field,

which a man **found**
and covered up;

then **in his joy**
he goes and sells

all that he has

and buys that agricultural
field."

- Matthew 13:44

Chapter 1

Humanity; God's Eternal Love-Dream!

I am so glad that we have a gospel that can be measured geographically in a global context.

Listen; if the gospel we represent does not at least include the uttermost parts of the earth, then there is something wrong with our gospel and we need to discover the gospel that does.

Ha... ha... ha...

God has never had less in mind than *what He has always been mindful of.*

It is the human race that carries *the very focus of God's heart.*

Humanity is God's eternal *love-dream.*

When the man who found the treasure in Matthew 13:44, hid the treasure again, *and then went away and sold all that he had* **to buy the whole field**...

(Remember Jesus said that the kingdom of heaven is like a treasure hidden in an agricultural field)

...Now that man who *found the treasure* **immediately calculated a value equal to all that he had,** because his intent was to reveal, not to leave the treasure hidden, **but *to reveal the original value of that treasure, and thus also the field it is buried in!***

Now in our understanding of that scripture in Matthew 13, up to that point no one found the treasure, but the man who does show up on the scene and find the treasure is none other than *the man, Jesus Christ.*

Because you see, in his incarnate being, the man, Jesus Christ *is the full representation of the invisible God.*

The word *"incarnate"* is a Latin word meaning: **In The Flesh.**

So; in the LOGOS becoming flesh, in the WORD *finding its completeness* ...In the prophetic word which we have a volume of in our Old Covenant Scriptures, *finding its completeness* ...you see, that whole prophetic context of Scripture ***pointed to this person; to the man, Jesus Christ!***

That whole Old Covenant portion, that whole prophetic context of the Old Testament Scripture *pointed to this person, to this moment,* ***when the eternal intent of God will be fully clothed in flesh;*** *in human skin* *"...**unveiling**,"* says Paul in Colossians 2:9, within that human body, *"the **fullness** of Deity."*

Jesus did not come to give us a different angle on God, you know, a different side of God, the happy side of God, *but watch out for His dark side.*

Ha... ha... ha... No!

Jesus came to <u>unveil</u> *the spectacular God!*

His younger brother James *who eventually got the light*

...Remember there was a time when none of Jesus' brothers followed Him.

...So if you feel sometimes a little isolated in your various communities and wherever you are, feeling that, you know, I am saying something very profound here now, which is perhaps confusing people, because of their current beliefs they are clinging to ...listen, **don't worry about it. You are in good company still!**

...Some of them will come around eventually, just like Jesus' own family did.

Because; as you can well remember form Scripture: There was a time in Jesus' ministry where not only his brothers, *but even his own mother stood outside.* John 7:5 makes it plain that *"none of his brothers believed in him."*

But, glory hallelujah, His younger brother James *did eventually get it!*

Paul mentions this fact in 1 Corinthians 15.

Remember where Paul speaks about how Jesus appeared to several individuals after His resurrection. And at one point Paul says, *"He even appeared to a group of about 500 people at once, most of whom were still alive at the time when Luke wrote about it."*

He says, *"...and then He also appeared to James."*

Can you imagine that encounter? Can you just imagine when James, the younger brother of Jesus, who knew Jesus, like Paul did, *after the flesh, or according to the flesh; from a human point of view* ...that same James who was at that time a part of the outsider group, you know, the group who questioned whether this brother of theirs could really be the Messiah of God ...*can you even imagine* **that encounter between that James and the resurrected Jesus?**

I am so glad that Jesus didn't come to win a debate of words and doctrine and theology.

He is *perfect theology!*

Ha... ha... ha...

He is: **THEO - LOGOS!**

He is **the very logic of God!**

So, when John begins his own writing, when he is himself already more than 90 years old, he starts with: *"In the beginning..."*

Not in the beginning when John and his friends and fellow disciples first began to understand the gospel, ha... ha... ha... no, but *way back in the beginning,* meaning: Before Abraham was, before Adam was, *was the Word; the LOGOS.*

And the destiny of that LOGOS was always *to become flesh!*

And so, when Jesus introduces us to the God of creation, He introduces Him as **our ABBA; our Father, our Papa.**

He says: *"If you've seen Me, you've seen the Father!"*

You see; *the revelation of Jesus Christ is the revelation of: the FATHER.*

Jesus didn't come to give us a neat little 5 point detailed doctrine.

He came to make the invisible God *visible!*

He came to make Him *known!*

He came to *unveil* the Father.

He came to show us *who He really is!*

...And you see; His Spirit of Truth, His precious Holy Spirit, *bears such immediate witness, such intimate witness, to who God really is, when He cries out, and announces from* <u>*within us*</u>*: ABBA, or Father;* <u>*Daddy*</u> *God!*

So, in the book of James 1:17...

...Now remember this is that same James we are talking about; *this is now Jesus' own younger brother, James,* who now gets to write down his own account.

In the context of that same chapter, James chapter 1, (which was written and distributed to all the churches in the midst of great contradiction), remember how he starts of saying: *"Count it all joy brethren when you meet with and are faced with various contradictions."* (He is writing to the scattered tribes, they have lost their lands). He concludes that chapter with addressing the widows and the orphans, *those who have faced the most severe contradictions in life;* **they have lost their whole identity, their national identity, even their identity as people,** and so he counts it a privilege to introduce them in verse 17 *to* **that** **"'Father of light itself;' the constant One, with whom there is no variableness – no fickle instability ...no shifting shadows due to change!"** ...**Emphasizing and concluding for them that** **God does not have a dark side!**

We live in an age where there are so many things changing; there are so many changes happening all at once. Our younger generations are growing up in a world where everything changes all the time. The only constant thing that can be relied on is *change!*

But, hey, thank God for a Jesus that is **the same,** yes, ***even* today and *forever!*** He is even the same yesterday, even as far back as you can replay yesterday. ***His sameness continues from eternity to eternity!***

Ha... ha... ha... Hallelujah! Thank you God for that reality! What a wonderful thing!

You see, and it is in that sameness that *He has come to introduce us to an* <u>eternal</u> *knowledge; to a proper understanding,* so that we may <u>fully know</u> *even as we have always been known.*

Growing up in Africa we used to sing a song called: Oh Lord remember me! And we used to sing that same line over and over and over till ad nauseam. And then, years later, I was supposed to preach in a little village in Malawi, and they were singing that same old song again, and when it was finally my turn to get up and speak I had the privilege of getting up and announcing to them: Hey, *I think we've got our song wrong!* Ha... ha... ha...

I took them to Psalm 8 where David writes and he says: *"What is Man that You are **Mind-full** of him?"*

You see sometimes we try and translate Adam's fall to a time where God kind of got out of touch with us, and lost track of the human race, *and somehow forgot us and our existence down here on planet earth.*

I am so glad *it wasn't actually God who did the hiding away in the garden.*

Listen; **the Shepherd never forsook the sheep!**

We all, like sheep, have gone astray; *not God!*

I am so glad God is not missing in action; *God is never lost!*

You see; **we don't have to talk God into doing things for us.**

Sometimes we get our prayers so wrong. We've got this idea that we have got to really storm the gates of heaven, because you know, God is so reluctant you see, He is really reluctant sometimes, you know, especially on certain days of the week, and it is on those days you've got to really beat down heaven's door to try and win just a glimmer of attention, to try and feel just a goose-bump at least. And then on some days, *'Boy oh boy, did you feel Him today; wasn't He just so close!'*

Ha... ha... ha... Hey, I've got news for you: **God is bigger than your feelings!**

Listen; **nothing that you do can get you any closer to God than you already are!**

Nothing that God can do can possibly get Him any closer to you either!

...Because; in the incarnation, the Father of lights removed the veil, and broke into this physical dimension, He came into our world with <u>the true light</u> that enlightens everyone.

In Jesus Christ God *announces* **a new horizon;** *a change of scenery!* **He announces that** *a new day has dawned!*

Now everything is seen in a new light!

Peter writes and he says: *"You will do well to pay attention to this as to light shining in a dark place."*

...And he was speaking of the prophetic account, but he says, *'But let's not give the prophetic account such prominence in our reference* **that it becomes another veil that blindfolds us again, and keeps us in the dark and hides us from <u>seeing</u> the day that has dawned!'**

Where has the day dawned? *"In our hearts!"*

In 2 Corinthians 4:6 Paul said,

"It's the God who said: 'Let light shine out of darkness' **that have shone into our hearts***..."*

Listen; **your heart is the very target of God!**

He always aims for your heart, not your head!

So hang in there if you feel like you can't quite keep up with what's being said, in your grasping of it, and that so much is being said that is a little over your head, or beyond what you thought you knew and understood; hey, *we are not aiming for your head!*

Ha... ha... ha...

We have wasted so much time and so many years trying to get revelation knowledge to drop down from our think tank into our hearts.

Listen it's the wrong direction; it's the wrong way round!

God always impacts out hearts first *and our minds eventually catches up, with a deeper understanding,* of that reality our spirits have already grasped and embraced and know.

It's never an in-pouring, it's always an outpouring! *It's out of your innermost being*...

Ha... ha... ha... Hallelujah!

So, the God who said: *"**Let** light shine **out of** darkness..."* (Wow, what a reputation He has. Because, He created light in Genesis, before

28

He even created the suns and the moons. He said: *"Light **be!**"* and so light **is!**)

Now, that same God who spoke the universe into existence **is the very One** *who shone into our hearts* **to give the light** *of the knowledge of* **the glory** *of God*

Where is that glory?

*...**In the very face of man.***

Where did God reveal it to us?

In the man: **Jesus Christ!**

In the person of Jesus Christ *God defines GLORY.*

Both *His glory* and *our glory* are defined there!

And Jesus unveils and reveals it to be the same GLORY, amen; *inseparable!*

Do you remember what God says in Isaiah 40?

*"All flesh **shall see it** ...together."*

As you read this book **and comprehend** I declare to you prophetically that **the tsunami wave of God's glory that is braking through into your heart and dawning on your consciousness like a shaft of light *is about to sweep over your communities!***

29

In our fellowship in the gospel we are participating in the most unstoppable force; the most unstoppable influence known in the universe!

Light always dispels darkness. *There is no competition or combat there!*

Paul says in Colossians 1 that *"God delivered us out of the dominion of darkness **by bringing us into His marvelous light!"***

So, let me ask a question. What gave darkness dominion over us, *if darkness is not a force in and of itself, but **merely the absence of light**?*

Darkness only finds its dominion in our ignorance!

So, how did God address *our ignorance; our darkness?*

According to Colossians 1:13 **He has totally done away with *anything that could possibly distance our minds* from His eternal truth, from eternal REALITY; from HIM, *through the veil of sin-consciousness!***

He has done away with it all; He has totally done away with *the veil of sin-unconscious* that has kept us blindfolded and that has blinded us for so long!

And now in Jesus Christ He displays His glory *in the face of a man!*

30

Colossians 1:15 makes it clear that *"He, Jesus, is the exact image; the very likeness, of the invisible God"*

He makes God *visible* and *unveils* Him to us! He is GOD *revealed* in flesh!

God cannot ever become invisible again!

Emanuel (God with us; *in us*) can never be Emanuel without you!

Because the destiny of the Word was *flesh!*

The Word *became* flesh!

In many of our translations we read: *"The Word became flesh ...and dwelt **amongst** us."* But the Greek clearly states that, *"**The Word became flesh and dwelt <u>in</u> us,**"* not **amongst** us, but **within us!**

It's funny how we always play for a little bit of distance.

God has come to tabernacle. He has come to dwell *...in human form ...for all eternity.*

And now Paul writes in Colossians 2:9 and he says:

*"The **fullness** of the Godhead; the **fullness** of Deity **dwelt in Him, in Jesus, in bodily form...**"*

Can you imagine the **completeness** of God?

We are not talking about a percentage of our understanding, a percentage of our theology, of our doctrines, of our encounters, and our experiences.

No, **the fullness; *God in completeness* came to dwell in bodily form, in the man, Jesus Christ, *in whose face <u>we discover</u> the light of life*.**

He is the One who shines into our hearts to give us an understanding, *an accurate understanding,* wherein <u>the veil is removed</u> and wherein <u>distance is canceled</u> in its every ugly definition!

In the incarnation; in Jesus Christ, God revealed that *He has forever married the human race!*

Hey, the incarnation was not just a temporary thing!

God's oneness with Man is *permanent!*

The man, Jesus Christ, is forever seated at, and in, and as, the right hand of the Father, as an eternal testimony to the reality that *God has forever associated and united Himself with the human race!*

We are seated in the heavenly realm itself in oneness with the Godhead!

Our life is hidden with Christ in the very bosom of the Father!

Chapter 2

Eternal Reality Unveiled!

Did you know that if you can take and stretch out just the veins in your body they could span the globe twice? That statement puts both the human body and the globe in a different perspective, doesn't it? You are reading, and we are having a discussion together in the gospel, here in this book, even though I might be in the USA and you could be located just about anywhere on this planet, yet we are sharing the same thoughts, and we are in fellowship together right now.

You see; **distance is a perspective, it is merely a perspective in our minds.**

I am so glad that He has come to give us understanding that *He has removed every possible definition of <u>distance</u>!*

We celebrate today a gospel that introduces not just closeness, but <u>*oneness*</u>!

"In Him we live, and move, and have our being ...our I am-ness" - Acts 17:28

That's what that Greek word means there in Colossians 2:10, *"Our I am-ness is discovered there in Him!"*

Ha... ha... ha... Oh hallelujah!

Paul says, Colossians 2, verse 9 & 10, *"In Him, in Jesus, dwelt the <u>fullness</u> of Deity, in bodily form, and our <u>completeness</u>, our I am-ness is revealed there in Him as well."*

Therefore *our <u>completeness</u> is discovered there in our I am-ness,* **as our I am-ness is** **explored** **there in Him;** *in oneness with him!*

So, in the gospel we have come to celebrate the I am-ness of Man; *Man's oneness with God, <u>unveiled</u>, in God the Son,* and we have also come to celebrate the I am-ness of God, *<u>unveiled</u>, in ordinary human life.*

I am so glad we are no longer in the days of the great big-shot preachers behind a great big pulpit, and here we are, just reduced to audience, in yet another great big conference. *Those days are over!* **Because** *you* **are what it's all about!**

The message of the gospel is all about you! Because, you see, Jesus was not in trouble; *He didn't need saving!*

We were in trouble; *we needed the saving!*

So, we can very politely and religiously say, *'But it's all about Jesus,'* **and then we somehow think we give Jesus the goose-bumps when we say that. But no no, Jesus says,** *'Hey guys, when are you going to get it? I'm all about you!'*

You see; Jesus did not come to compete with our little philosophies. He didn't come as a new product on the religious market, so we can have yet another option to choose from. He didn't come to perhaps win a few votes for the Christian cause. His mission was and is far larger than that!

Listen; *He came to put all of our religions out of business!*

He came to unveil something of far greater significance *than any religion could possibly offer!*

He did not come to confirm our religious beliefs; *He simply came to unveil ETERNAL REALITY!*

Remember that little lady who came to Jacob's well; who came to get a drink from Jacob's well and do her worship there on those sacred mountains, **Jesus came and unveiled to her a well of much greater significance!**

He began to unveil to her, to introduce to her a well *that is much closer to her* than the distance she had to travel from her village to that historic religious site.

It is great to be able to travel to the land of Israel from time to time, but hey, *don't go there for the anointing that hangs around in Israel.*

Listen; **the anointing hangs around in you!**

YOU are God's address!

You cannot get *any closer to God* if you try!

You cannot get any closer to God *than what He already is to you!*

God cannot get closer to mankind than what He already did, in the man, Jesus Christ; when the Word became flesh!

God cannot get any closer to mankind than when that word *concerning the Word that became flesh* finds an audience in us, and our hearts get impacted <u>by His love and by His nearness</u>, ignited with understanding, *to know Him* who is <u>true</u>, *and then suddenly also we see reflected in Him, ourselves.*

We are *IN HIM* who is <u>true</u>.

In the conclusion of Jesus' ministry in John 14:20 He said: *"In that day **you will <u>know</u>** that I am <u>in</u> My Father..."*

How did He get there?

Through our knowing?

No. **He has always been there!**

But you know what our <u>knowing</u> does do for us; *we discover that **we too are <u>in</u> Him** who is true, and that **He is <u>in</u> us.***

Wow! Hallelujah!

36

Allow the Holy Spirit to **awaken your understanding** to where you already are located geographically, *not in the flesh, but in the spirit,* amen.

A lot of South African gold is hidden underground in bank faults in Zürich, Switzerland still today.

What happens to that gold during the process of being mined somewhere in South Africa or elsewhere in the world, and weighed, and transported, and then hidden in those bank vaults in Zürich, Switzerland, *where it will in all reality **never remain hidden?***

It becomes currency! It cannot be hidden <u>again</u> once it has become currency, and that is exactly what happens to that gold once discovered, *its value is accurately measured and established, and then it becomes <u>unstoppable currency</u>!*

Can you imagine the sheer volume of industry that is sustained globally by gold hidden in bank vaults not only in Zürich, Switzerland, but in bank vaults all over the world?

Can you imagine the amount of commerce and the amount of traffic that is sponsored by it at this very moment, whether it is by highway, aircraft, rail, or boat? No matter what line of research you conduct as far as the global economy is concerned, *you will always find a little thread, a link to that gold.* **Today that gold fuels only *a small portion* of the global**

**economy, but *a portion* none the less; it's
the very energy behind its share of a *mobile
world.*** For some it is the very source behind
the phrase: ***Hustle and bustle.***

Ha... ha... ha...

Now let me just add here quickly that no one
really knows exactly when the use of
commodity money was invented, but it has
been discovered that more than 5,000 years
ago already a primitive form of commodity
money were used in Mesopotamia, and it's
also been over 3,000 years already since metal
coins began circulating.

Now as far as history goes, future historians
will probably be dumbfounded when they look
back at our current world economic situation
and wonder in amazement at *how long the
people of our day allowed **worthless,
unsupported fiat paper** to pass as money.*

For more than 99% of recorded human
civilization, *money actually meant
something* ...right up until 1933 when
President Franklin D. Roosevelt untied the U.S.
Dollar from the Gold Standard, *and the rest of
the nations followed suit.*

The U.S. continued to allow foreign
governments to exchange their dollars for gold
if they so choose until 1971, when President
Richard Nixon abruptly ended the practice, *to
stop dollar-flush foreigners from sapping U.S
gold reserves even further.*

Switzerland was the last country to do away with the Gold Standard in 1999.

Today not a single one of the nations of this world base their currencies on gold, **although, gold mining does still have the most substantial impact on growth and wealth creation in developing countries such as South Africa, Mongolia and others;** Its effect is greatest in Papua New Guinea (15% of GDP), followed by Ghana (8% of GDP) and Tanzania (6% of GDP). **For these developing nations gold is also a major source of export and, therefore, foreign exchange earnings.**

Since the industrial revolution and the development of our world, culminating in the modern age we live in, *the output of goods and services grew faster than gold supplies could keep up with,* and so the world abandoned the Gold Standard and began to base their economies merely on the faith and good will of their governments, and their people, and upon the strength of their companies, and they began the practice of printing and putting more money into circulation every time a problem begins to develop.

(They supposedly do this to keep up with the growth, or to somehow hedge against inflation, which would drive down wages and stifle investment, and worst case scenario, would lead to another great depression).

Of course no one wants that, *so we all just keep printing and spending money like drunken sailors, or like it is going out of fashion or something!* And indeed it is!

This practice of printing money at will, has unfortunately led to **skyrocketing debt, runaway inflation, and great instability** in the markets, *and so everybody now lives **in fear of tomorrow.***

But nevertheless, *there is still hope,* regardless of what the naysayers and the doom-and-gloom guys want you to believe.

Right after the markets nearly collapsed in 2008, blockchain technology and cryptocurrency were invented and introduced in 2009, and are capable of producing stable inflation proof currencies, which could eventually be a suitable replacement for the Gold Standard.

So, the race is on to invent a viable cryptocurrency that could replace the U.S. dollar, or any other fiat paper currency for that matter, as the preferred reserve currency for global commerce.

That's right folks; we are on the verge of a major breakthrough and disruption in the financial markets, *for the betterment of a world **looking for better building blocks** to form **a new, more stable foundation** for a better tomorrow.*

Therefore you will soon see this new blockchain technology and cryptocurrency adopted in large scale, transforming all sorts of companies and governments from within, *as all the nations of the world, including the U.S.A, are desperately looking to* **stabilize** *their economies by reining in inflation and* **moving away from their by now practically useless overinflated fiat currencies.**

Thank God for *stable* **things which have** *lasting value!* Ha... ha... ha...

Such as *God's true gospel!*

What I want you to see and know is that the global financial revolution underway *is merely an outward sign, and a prophetic picture,* **pointing to a global revolution in religious beliefs,** *and a return to the true gospel of* **God** **already underway globally as well!**

Chapter 3

Discovering The Truth Sets You Free!

Paul says in Romans 1:19 that *"Whatever can be known of God **is manifest in Man.**"*

Oh, I know that verse 18 says that, *"Through their unrighteousness **they have suppressed the truth**."*

But that's not the point!

The real question is: **How long can you hide something that cannot remain hidden?**

The very mystery that once was hidden, says Paul in Colossians 1:27, that mystery *"which was hidden for ages and generations **has now been revealed.**"*

And then He tells us what that mystery is. He says: it is **Christ**...

Where?

Hiding somewhere in history, or perhaps in outer space somewhere, or somewhere off in the near or distant future, or in the sweet by-and-by?

No!

Christ ...**in the nations.**

Christ ...in **you**, *where He has been hiding all along.*

You see; **Gold does not become gold once it is discovered!**

No. Gold has been gold all along!

But why must it be discovered?

So that it can become *currency!*

So often people would want to look at this glorious Gospel of God; this almost-too-good-to-be-true message we preach, they want to look at it from a mere doctrinal, theological, point of view, and simply think, *'Well, it sounds to me like these guys are just preaching a universal gospel;* ***it's just universalism!'***

And so they somehow form the idea that we are saying that *'Everybody has got it, and everybody's okay,'* and so they ask: *'If that is the case then why bother?'*

And I absolutely agree with them! I mean; why even bother preaching the gospel then ***if*** *everybody is okay?*

Let me ask you, *is everybody okay?*

It doesn't seem like it to me!

44

All you have to do is turn on your television or look at your local newspaper to see that everybody is not okay.

But hey, listen carefully now: We DO carry an understanding that includes our neighborhood, and includes our continent, and all the other continents and islands of the world. Even the remotest parts of our planet! The most isolated people groups *are all included* **in what we have come to understand and know** *about the human race,* **according to what Father God Himself has revealed and restored to every single one of us in Jesus Christ!**

The whole human race, **they are all equally valued,** and *therefore they are also all equally included* **in the truth** *revealed in the gospel,* **in order to be rescued by it** *from the dominion of darkness,* which is nothing other than merely **a dominion of *ignorance*** – *not knowing* **the truth!**

So again: Is everyone saved in Christ's work of redemption?

YES THEY ARE!

But, is everybody okay? *Is everybody rescued?*

NO.

It takes the proclamation and or comprehension of the truth of the gospel to be rescued from the dominion of ignorance,

from the dominion of darkness; from that very *power* that holds people in bondage and causes people to live and experience a life less than what they were actually designed for!

Hence, *"You shall **discover** the truth and **that truth (you now know) shall set you free!"*** - John 8:32

For so many wasted years we have merely cultivated our land, the top-soil, you know, entertaining the flesh ...*the earthen vessel* ...**which carries the treasure!**

And yet, the treasure has been there all along, even though it has been largely overlooked.

***It has only remained hidden to us through our ignorance;* it has remained hidden from view through our misguided focus on the top-soil.**

I am so glad that this is just the first book in our series, *"The Gospel in 3-D!"* because I still have so much I want to reveal and make known to you, but let's just go to 2 Corinthians 4.

Oh boy, that is such a gloriously dangerous chapter, because it has chapter 3 just before it and chapter 5 written right after it... ha... ha... ha...

Oh my Jesus, this is just so beautiful!

46

You know, sometimes I almost wish we didn't even have to talk or write, *and we can all just sit and gaze together at where we are seated in Christ*

*...and just allow that veil, **which is an illusion anyway to begin with,** to just be **done away with for good, once and for all!***

*...So that we, **with unveiled faces,** may now together, individually, **behold Him <u>as in a mirror</u>***

*...**and therefore behold ourselves also there in Him; in His glory***

*...**and behold His glory in us***

*...**Him in me, and I in Him!***

I want to encourage you, wherever you are, right where you are, right here and now, in your beingness, I want to encourage you **to lift up your spiritual eyes and *to see a harvest that is already ripe within you, inside you, and within your neighbor, and within the nations as well; to see the finished work of Christ <u>in context</u>.***

It is finished is not a prophecy; *it is a reality!*

It is finished!

And so now, *God owes us nothing!*

And you know what, **now we owe Him nothing either!**

There is no rule-book, no law of requirements *that can match this kind of love!*

Law is outdated, *once romance begins!*

Just last month I was preaching up in New Hampshire and in Massachusetts in the U.S.A. and a brother came up to me after one of our sessions and said: *'No, no, no, really brother Rudi, it's a little difficult for me to agree with you when you say* **we owe God nothing,** *come on man,* **we owe Him everything!***'*

The answer I gave him came forth from the anointing; it was inspired, fresh from the Holy Spirit. I said to him,

'Imagine how your wife would offend you, if you had just bought her the most expensive **gift as an expression of your deep love for her,** *and* **yet** *she proceeds to offer to* **trade, or sell you something** *for the* **gift!***'*

You see; **Reward language, which is the language of religion,** *becomes so totally disarmed* **by** <u>gift</u> **language!**

<u>Gift</u> **language is the language of** *love!* God's not come *to buy favor from us;* **He has come to reveal favor to us!**

He has come to reveal *value!*

48

Why do I say that?

Because the man who **found** the treasure *and understands its true value and worth*, hid it again, **for us to discover!** - Matthew 13:44.

But let me just get back to 2 Corinthians 4, and I am quoting to you from the Mirror Bible.

Just as a side note: It is important for us to understand that when Paul wrote that letter to the Corinthians, known to us as 2 Corinthians or Second Corinthians, he did not write in Chapter and verse; *it was a letter, a conversation.*

You see, he is engaged in this conversation with the saints and so in Chapters 3 *he records* **the glory of God,** *compared to the fading glory of the flesh;* (Like the flower of the fields that has its moments and then the season is over for it, and it has to just kind of shrivel up and die again). You see, Paul speaks of **an unfading glory,** and he goes on to say in Chapter 3 verse 18, *"...which **we now behold; all of us do**..."*

So by the way; the Greek word for glory, DOXA, is an estimation of value term, and it comes from the word DOKAO, which means: OPINION.

That means every single individual on planet earth enjoys exactly the same access reference to the same opinion, to the same idea, because God is not our idea, **we are His** idea! *And He has given substance to the glory of His idea.*

The very intent, the very OPINION of God is now unveiled in human form, in the flesh, *where we can all see it together.*

Paul says, *"We __all__, with unveiled faces, are now beholding; we find ourselves gazing at, the glory of the Lord, __as in a mirror__."*

Hey that word, GLORY is such a rich word; it includes not only the OPINION and INTENT and FAVOR of God, but it includes also *His very CHARACTOR and SPIRIT, His Divine NATURE and SHEKINAH GLORY; the very PERSON and POWER of God!*

Listen; The days of window shopping the promises are over!

The days of crossing your fingers and hoping for better, perhaps tomorrow or in the future, are over!

We have wasted so many sincere but ignorant hours, days, months, years, trying to get THERE, *when "THERE" is where we __ARE__ to begin with!*

Now I know that that throws out most of our popular doctrine, and that makes people nervous.

Why?

Because religion needs paying and returning customers you see; they need *in-completion, a never ending journey!*

Religion thrives on two lies:

1. The illusion of **distance**, and
2. The illusion of **delay**.

That means you have to continue to strive to get THERE, *and because you didn't quite make it THERE this week, you have to come back again next week.*

Imagine if Jesus said that to the women at the well, do you think He would have made any lasting impact upon her life? *No, He would not have!*

Can you just imagine Him saying to her, *'I'm just going to give you a little taste of the real water of life ...but don't let it become a fountain in you, because then you'll become independent of Me, and I just can't have that you see!'*

Ha.... ha... ha...

Hey no man! Jesus didn't make it about himself, *He showed people the way to the Father;* **He introduced oneness with the Father!**

Listen, if the gospel we preach does not make people independent of us *then we are not preaching the gospel!*

According to Paul, in 2nd Corinthians 2:12; how do you measure successful ministry?

You measure successful ministry by how absent you preach yourself!

He says, *"Not only in my presence, **but much more in my absence,** discover **the full extent** of **your** salvation!"*

Wow, what an adventure!

Hey listen I want this series of books to just be a celebration of that adventure of life in Christ Jesus! And then I also want it to just become that launching pad for you to go and explore more on your own, *and discover for yourself the measureless dimensions **of the love of God,** and life more abundantly with Him; **in oneness with Him**

...I want you to be so free, and to feel so free *to go and explore for yourself, and discover on your own, **the compelling influence of the love of God;** the depth of it, the height, the length of it, the width of that AGAPE of God, *demonstrated in Christ, which **surpasses knowledge!***

*"...**much more** in my absence!"*

*"**For it is God who is at work within you, both to will and to do of His good pleasure!"***
- Philippians 2:13

So in the context of what Paul just said about our unveiled encounter, this is what I declare over our time together in this series of books: An **unveiled** *encounter!*

Because we all are beholding the same reference: The glory of the Lord, *AS IN A MIRROR.*

And we are together discovering the same METAMORPHE – a realignment of our thoughts – away from (The Greek word is the word, APO – away from) the glory that defined us before to the *unfading glory of His presence and of His image and likeness.*

And so now, with that new understanding, and with us discovering our lives in Christ; *the fullness we enjoy there,* can you just imagine what our fellowship and our getting together now *becomes?!*

Ha... ha... ha...

Hey, the very word, *"CHURCH gathering"* *takes on new dimensions then!*

Chapter 4

Joint Seeing

So, getting to 2 Corinthians 4 in the Mirror Bible, Paul says, in verse 2,

*"We have renounced **hidden agendas**..."*

The hidden agendas Paul is referring to here, is people's efforts of employing a little bit of the law in an attempt to supposedly *"balance out"* grace.

He says, *"We have distanced ourselves from any obscure craftiness to try and manipulate God's Word* (the gospel) **to make it mean what it does not say!**"

He goes on to say, *"With truth on open display in us, we highly recommend our lives* (we recommend the source of our life and joy – God and His gospel) *to every person's conscience!"*

The word, *"conscience"* is a Latin term and it means: **To discover together,** *or* **to know together,** but in the Greek the word is, SUNEIDO, and it translates as: ***joint seeing.***

It is also interesting to note that ***joint seeing*** is the exact opposite of HADES – **not to see.**

Paul goes on to say that, *"Truth finds its most authentic and articulate expression in human life."* With this the apostle John, in John 1, concurs when he talks a bout the word becoming flesh, because it then becomes the enlightenment of every person.

Paul then says, *"This beats any doctrinal debate!"*

The Mirror Bible may read a little different from the regular translations, but it's because it is a paraphrased translation taken directly from the original text. The author concluded his paraphrase of Paul's words in 2 Corinthians 4:2 as saying: *"It is our passion for all to see what is so completely obvious in the mirror of our redeemed likeness and innocence!"*

Paul says in verse 3,

"If our message seems vague to anyone, it is not because we are withholding something from them! **It is just because some are so stubborn in their efforts to uphold an outdated religious belief and resulting religious system that they don't see it!**

They are all equally found in Christ, but they prefer to remain lost in the cul-de-sac language of the law!"

Paul says, *"We are not employing, as so many others do, a little bit of law in an attempt to "balance out" or worse yet, "neutralize" grace!"*

Paul says, *"We have in fact distanced ourselves from anything, from any teaching that would try to manipulate **God's Word** **(God's gospel)** to make it mean what it does not say!"*

The author of the Mirror Bible wrote a little chapter as an introduction to understanding The Holy Bible, called: **Understanding the incarnation code,** and if you want to get the Paraphrased Mirror Translation just for that, then I encourage you to do it, *because what gives context to Scripture is not our interpretation that we have evolved and come into over many generations.* No. **There is only one accurate eternal context to Scripture: The whole book is about Jesus, *and the whole of Jesus is about you!***

Jesus himself said at one point, *"It is good that you study the Scriptures so diligently, but if you have missed the fact that it's about Me; if you have missed Me in all of it, you have missed the point!"* - John 5:39-40

He has come to unveil Scripture in its most radical, tangible, beautiful, *full context:* **your skin!**

The best leather covered Mirror Bible or any other kind of Bible you can ever get is **your skin**

*...it is tailor made for the **fullness of Deity** to dwell in and to be expressed in!*

(Paul says as much in Colossians 2:9 & 10, he concludes with *"...__you are__ complete in Him!*)

You see God didn't just leave us out of this deal; He didn't leave us out in the cold, not included, as if, you know, *the fullness of God __dwells in Jesus,__* and we just salute and adore *that fullness of God* in wonderful Jesus Christ!

I mean, *Jesus Christ would then be reduced to merely a historic icon,* if that was indeed all that God said in Jesus.

But, I am so glad that the single grain of wheat did not abide alone, it fell into the earth, died, *and in its resurrection brought forth its abundant harvest!*

That is why in summery Jesus said in various places, *"I want you to lift up your spiritual eyes and see how white the harvest is. __It is fully ripe!__ Do not say 'There are four more months and __then__ comes the harvest,' listen, __you are looking at the wrong harvest!__ That one is going to disappoint again. The bread that __you labor for__ will not feed you, __but the true bread from heaven does!__"*

He has come *"__As an open statement of the truth, in your skin,__ written not with ink, or chiseled in stone, but __engraved within your inner being, by the Spirit of the living God himself...__"*

Listen God has so much to say to the world, *__wrapped up in your skin!__*

Missionaries we are indeed, but in a new context, not in the letter of the law, *perpetuating that old system of guilt and shame and condemnation and fear and nothing but death.*

So, missionaries we are indeed, *but in the newness of the Spirit,* **promoting the Christ-life within; the indwelling Spirit!**

We are simply unveiling the most relevant conversation!

The mystery unveiled <u>as in a mirror</u>!

Some very concerned well know church leaders here in the U.S.A. are writing in some very popular Christian magazines, warning against a supposed *radical extreme grace message.*

But you see **the problem has never been to *exaggerate* grace, the problem has always been to *under-estimate such a great salvation.***

God does not get nervous when we extravagantly talk about His love!

Because Paul says, *"**It surpasses knowledge!**"*

His love *awakens you* from within! The dimensions of the AGAPE of God *surpass knowledge and it awakens our hearts to Him!!*

Paul says, *"With truth on open display in us, we highly recommend our **life** to everyone's **conscience!**"*

I want to emphasize again that word: *"**conscience**."*

Is *"conscience"* an English word or a Latin word?

"Conscience" is not an English word, but it's a word we borrowed from the Latin. And that is one that is allowed in the Bible, not so with that other Latin word: *"penance."*

That word *'"penance"* does not belong in the Bible.

We have inherited that Latin word, *"penance"* from our old church fathers who thought, *'Hey, we can make a lot of money by making people feel guilty.'*

And then they thought, *'*

You know, maybe it's a good idea to just add a "re" in front of that word "penance" to set up a belief-system that perpetuate the idea of fines and payment for indulgences in sin, you know, to soothe their guilt-ridden souls temporarily, while we keep making a lot of money.'

They basically resurrected the old sacrificial system of the Old Covenant, but with a new twist; they just changed it a little bit.

Listen; *"Repentance"* is not a valid Greek word.
It is not found in the Greek anywhere.

The real Greek word used is: METANOIA, but
we will get into that maybe a little later on; or in
one of the other books in this series.

The word *"conscience"* however is a valid Latin
word, because Paul wrote in Greek and he
used the word SUNEIDO

The Latin term con-science or con-scientia is
made up of two words: "con" meaning
together and "science" or "scientia" meaning:
to discover; to see or know

SUN-EIDO is exactly the same term in Greek
as the term CON-SCIENCE in Latin.

SUNEIDO means: *to know together or, to
see together; joint seeing.*

Which by the way is exactly the opposite of the
word HADES or HA-EIDES.

HA is a negative term meaning: *not,* and
IDEIN or EIDO meaning: *to see*

Thus the word SUNEIDO means: *to see
together,* and the word HADES means: *not
to see.*

**The gospel is an open statement of the
truth – proclaiming *that Jesus has come as
an open statement of the truth himself
clothed in your skin!* Isn't that just beautiful?!**

*...**Written not with ink but with the Spirit of the Living God, not on tablets of stone either, but on the tablets of the heart – <u>it is a knowledge that is already engraved in your inner-being</u>!***

You see your spirit-man already knows this truth *and bears witness with it* in your own heart!

In Jesus, God *unveiled* the most relevant conversation!

And thus, in the gospel also, that same mystery is *unveiled.*

I say again: **God has so much to say to the world, *wrapped up in your skin!***

The mystery *unveiled* ...<u>*as in a mirror*</u>!

What a privilege we have, what an opportunity just to be able to share with people **the good news conversation, the mystery *revealed,*** *and to be able to watch their faces and see their eyes ignite with the light of life!*

You see we carry a gospel *that **belongs** to every person on this planet!*

We know something about the next individual that most of them do not know about themselves. What a privilege, *what joy! What **wealth** we are entrusted with!*

Thank you Jesus!

62

So, *"With truth on open display in us, we highly recommend our lives to everyone's* **conscience** (everyone's **joint seeing** *and* **joint discovery***)"* - 2 Corinthians 4:2

You know in Africa it is quite popular to go on safari as a group, and I still remember how my wife Carmen and I was afforded the privilege to go on safari with my brother Danie and his wife Chantelle, right after their wedding. We were all so excited to be able to go on safari together in the Kruger National Game Reserve, *especially seeing that Carmen had never been to Africa,* and I remember how it struck me that **the whole point of the safari was to be able to include everyone in the group in the same sighting ...but especially Carmen.**

The idea is never for just the people on the right side of the vehicle to look at the Leopard up in the tree, and the people on the left, *'No sorry, you're only allowed to look at the Impala on the left.'* Ha... ha... ha... No!

The whole idea of the safari is *to find a sighting and then to do your best* **to give everyone in your group, the best possible vantage point, so that they can see for themselves ...but especially Carmen.**

And when we did happen upon a sighting it was our goal to point out exactly where the animal was, *so everyone could see it for themselves.* If someone perhaps still had a frown on their face *because they just did not see it yet,* we didn't become all frustrated at them and annoyed, looking down at our watches and saying, *'Well it's going to take them too long to see it, so, time's up! It's time to move on and go and get out of here!'*

No, no, no, *our whole concern was with that person who was **in the right place at the right moment, but they haven't seen it yet,** and so **we just pointed a little more accurately perhaps, or explained with a little more detailed direction** describing perhaps a little better, mere clearly, **exactly where the animal was**,* and then we didn't have to say or do much else, we just had to look at their eyes, **because you cannot hide it from your face when you finally do see it!**

It was such a joy to see their faces light up when they finally saw it for themselves, *but especially Carmen,* because she has never seen African wildlife in their natural habitat!

Hey, people do not go on safari to sit at the lodge and watch the latest and greatest National Geographic footage!

So often we have reduced Christian ministry to just that!

I am so glad you picked up this book and this series of books to read, but I am not inviting you into seeing what I see concerning the mystery of Christ, *to just simply entertain you with great teaching.*

Oh, don't get me wrong, I thank God for the entertainment value of what His Spirit communicates, *but that is not the point!*

Wow, ha... ha... ha... come on, **it's *your* moment!**

It's *your* time to shine *also!*

So, shine baby, *shine!*

The Holy Spirit's whole motivation in inspiring me to write these books, *and then inspiring you to read them,* **is to invite <u>you</u> into a place of mutual encounter, and therefore also a mutual unveiling of the same reality!**

So that we, together, as individual members of the whole human race, may *comprehend and see* ...so that we may *intimately know, even as we have always been known.*

Oh how patient God is with us, *while inviting us to see the same.*

It is always so wonderful after such a marvelous safari trip into the African wilderness to sit around the campfire and feel the excitement in the air as you listen to the spontaneous conversations, everyone sharing their photos, even of the same sighting, maybe from a little bit of a different angle, but it's the same Lion or Leopard, or perhaps Elephant or Rhino sighting everyone is so excited about and conversing over.

You see in that environment, the conversation is so natural, *because we have all enjoyed the same reference.*

We are still in 2nd Corinthians 4:2,

*"**Truth finds its most authentic and articulate expression in human life!**"* ...not in a wonderful building with a magnificent sound system, an acrylic pulpit, air conditioning, and all the modern conveniences

...Thank God for all of it, *but it's not the point!*

We gather together in buildings, *in an intimate environment of fellowship; it simply being a place of celebration and mutual discovery, so that we can ultimately find, **in human life,** in the nitty-gritty of day to day living, in society, in family, in business, in the marketplace, at school, or wherever we find ourselves spending our time, **we find new context** to a previously boring mundane existence; **the context of communicating and revealing** <u>**value**</u> **to others,** the context of SUNEIDO; **joint seeing!***

Paul says, *"**This beats any doctrinal debate!**"*

Listen; **avoid doctrinal debates! Especially on Facebook and other types of social media!**

Do not get tempted to get involved in trying to defend a doctrine, because let me tell

you straight, even if you win the argument, *you've lost a friend!*

There is something that beats, by far, the best doctrinal debate; *it's the <u>unveiling</u> of the <u>living</u> Christ <u>in you</u>!*

God has no other agenda! He has no *bigger agenda* for your life!

Many people want to know, *'I wonder what God's plan is for my life?'*

That's not important!

Do you want to know **what is important** then?

It is for you to know that **your *life* is His plan!**

Let me say that again: **Your life *is His plan!***

He is so excited about your life!

...about living life <u>with you</u>!

God is so excited about the gospel *alive in you!*

He is so excited about you; *He has given such context to you!*

In Jesus He has revealed *the ultimate you* to you!

God is excited about the *unveiling* of <u>Christ in you</u>!

...The <u>living</u> Christ, REAL and ON DISPLAY, in YOU!

Your life is His plan!

Chapter 5

The Treasure Within!

"If our message seems vague to anyone, it is not because we are withholding something from them! **It is just because some are so stubborn in their efforts to uphold an outdated system that they don't see it! They are all equally found in Christ, but they prefer to remain lost, in the cul-de-sac language of the Fall, and of the law!"* - 2nd Corinthians 4:3

The lost sheep, the lost coin, the lost son, they are all found, safe and sound, *in One Man; Jesus Christ!*

"The self-improvement programs, **kept alive by the survival efforts** *of both the social-political and religious systems of this world,* **veil the minds** *of the ignorant and unbelieving;* **exploiting their ignorance about their true origin and identity, and their redeemed innocence.** *The veil of ignorance and unbelief obstructs a person's view* **and keeps one from seeing what the light of the gospel so clearly reveals:** (and what is that?) **The glory of God; <u>the very image and likeness of our Maker, redeemed in human form</u> – this is exactly what the gospel of Jesus Christ is all about."* - 2nd Corinthians 4:4

Verse 5,

"Even though we recommend ourselves with great confidence..."

Remember, Paul said that he recommended his own **life** to every person's conscience.

He says that now with unveiled faces we behold the truth *and by an open statement of the truth,* says the Revised Standard Version, *we commend ourselves to every person's conscience.*

And oh, then some people will immediately say, *'No, no, no, you're putting too much emphasis on yourself; you're putting too much emphasis on Man.'*

So Paul just caters to them a little bit here in verse 5, he says,

"Even though we recommend ourselves with great confidence, it is not with arrogance; **we do not preach ourselves! We preach Christ Jesus the Lord;** *we are salvation junkies, personally employed –* **fully engaged and influenced** *by Jesus, for the sake of everyone else!"*

Verse 6, *"This light is sourced in the same God who said, "Light, be!" And thus light shone* **out of** *darkness!* **He lit the lamp in our understanding, so that we may clearly recognize the features of His likeness in the face of Jesus Christ, <u>reflected within us</u>.***"*

God introduces the truth of the gospel to us, *so that we may recognize **every detail of God's likeness** in the person of Jesus Christ **and realize** that what is revealed in Jesus **is also mirrored within us!***

The John Knox Translation of this same verse reads,

*"The same God who bade light shine **out of** darkness **has kindled a light in our hearts,** whose shining is **to make known His glory, as He has revealed it,** in the features of Jesus Christ."*

And what is revealed?

Verse 7,

*"We have discovered this treasure, **where it was hidden all along, in these frail skin-suits made of clay.** We take no credit for finding it there however. **Because it took the enormous power of God's love, in the achievement of Christ, <u>to rescue our minds</u>, and so also our very person, <u>from the very lies we believed</u>!"***

It is quite interesting to note that the Greek word for *"earthen vessel;" these skin-suits made of clay,* is: OYSTRAKINOS meaning: **the oyster**

Thus, these skin suits you and I live in **is the oyster that carries the pearl of great price!**

You see Paul wasn't going through some positive exercises of the mind, you know, trying to exercise his willpower when he said: *"From now on I am just going to try and think more positively about people ...until you irritate me enough to change my mind yet again about you!"*

Ha... ha... ha... No man!

Paul said, *"**I discovered and found something of the utmost value; I found something out about you <u>that is more true</u> than anything that you can possibly do, to distract me, <u>from what I see about you</u>. You see, I know who you <u>truly ultimately</u> are! And so, I am not going to allow any distraction, any contradiction to change my mind about you. I am not going to be tempted to waste another day knowing people according to the flesh, when I can more intimately know them according to spirit-reality, when I can truly know them according to the truth; <u>the truth as it is revealed in Jesus Christ</u>*!*"*

Remember: *Jesus was not an example for us, **but of us!***

Jesus has come to *unveil <u>us</u>*!

He has come to introduce <u>us</u> *to ourselves* again; *who we ultimately are!*

So that we may know ourselves, *even as we have always been known.*

We have this treasure *right here and now in earthen vessels!*

What an exciting adventure!

We thank you Father!

We thank you Lord!

I thank you Holy Spirit that we can spend our lives in the full focus, the full awareness of *the unveiled Christ **alive within us.***

Thank you Papa!

Thank you that we can now enjoy this place You have prepared for us Jesus; *a place of oneness, a place of resonance, a place of mutual knowing,* where the COINONIA, ***the intimate fellowship and life of our faith ignites,** through the acknowledging of every good thing **that is already within us,** in our eternal association, and union, and now oneness with Christ.*

Thank you precious Jesus!

Amen

In closing, I urge you to get yourself a copy of *"The Mirror Bible,"* it is the best paraphrase translation of the Scriptures from the original Greek that I have ever read, and it's available online at: www.amazon.com and several other book sellers.

If you want me or someone a part of our team to come to where you are, *anywhere in the world,* and give a talk or teach you and some of your friends *about the gospel message and these redemption realities,* simply contact us at www.livingwordintl.com

…or you can always find me, Rudi Louw, on www.facebook.com

If your life has changed as a result of reading this book, *please write to me and let me know.*

I would love to share in your joy,

…so that my joy in writing this series of books may be full!

"That which was **from the beginning,**

which we have heard
(with our spiritual ears),
which we have seen
(with our spiritual eyes),
which we have looked upon
(beheld, focused our attention upon),
and which our hands have also handled
(which we have also experienced),

concerning the Word of life,

we declare to you,

that you also may have this
fellowship with us;

and truly our fellowship is with
the Father
and with His Son Jesus Christ.

And these things we write to you
that your joy may be full."
                              ~ 1 John 1:1-4

About the Author

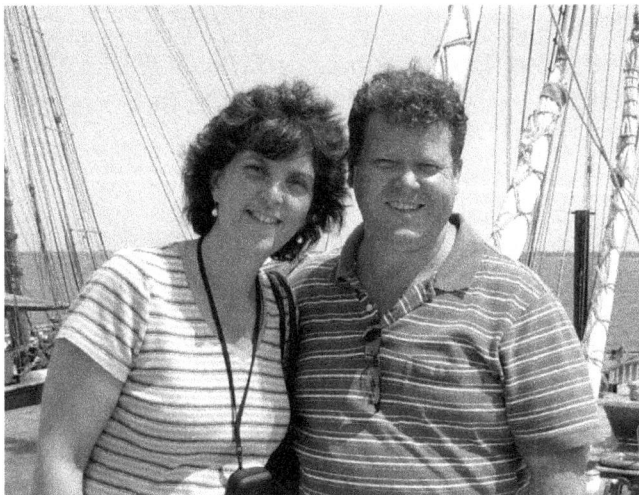

Rudi & Carmen Louw named their ministry: Living Word International. They love to travel and minister both locally and internationally.

Rudi was born and raised in the country of South Africa, while Carmen grew up in Cortland, New York.

They function in the ministry of reconciliation (2 Corinthians 5:18-21) and flow strongly with the Holy Spirit and His anointing to teach, preach, prophesy, heal, and whatever is needed to touch people's lives with the reality of God's love and power.

God has given them keen insight into what He has to say to mankind in Christ Jesus and the whole work of redemption, *concerning the revelation and restoration of* **humanity's true identity.**

Therefore, they emphasize THE GOSPEL, IN CHRIST REALITIES, the GRACE of God, the WORD OF RIGHTEOUSNESS, *and all such eternal truths essential to salvation and living the CHRIST-LIFE.*

They have been granted this wisdom and revelation into the knowledge of God, by the resurrected Spirit of Jesus Christ, *to establish and strengthen believers in the faith of God, and to activate them in ministering to others.*

Not only are people set free from the poison and bondage of sin, condemnation and all kinds of intimidation, (upheld, strengthened and reinforced by age old religious ideas born out of ignorance) **but many are brought into a closer more intimate relationship with Father God, as** *Daddy*, through accurate teaching and unveiling of the gospel message, prophetic words, healings and miracles.

Rudi & Carmen are closely knitted together with several other effective Christians, church fellowships, and groups of believers who share the same revelation and passion **to impart the truth of the gospel to others, so as to impact and transform the world we live in with the LOVE and POWER of God.**

www.ingramcontent.com/pod-product-compliance
Lightning Source LLC
Chambersburg PA
CBHW060653030426
42337CB00017B/2598